Dear Parent:
Your child's love of reading starts here!

Every child learns to read in a different way and at his or her own speed. Some go back and forth between reading levels and read favorite books again and again. Others read through each level in order. You can help your young reader improve and become more confident by encouraging his or her own interests and abilities. From books your child reads with you to the first books he or she reads alone, there are I Can Read Books for every stage of reading:

SHARED READING
Basic language, word repetition, and whimsical illustrations, ideal for sharing with your emergent reader

BEGINNING READING
Short sentences, familiar words, and simple concepts for children eager to read on their own

READING WITH HELP
Engaging stories, longer sentences, and language play for developing readers

READING ALONE
Complex plots, challenging vocabulary, and high-interest topics for the independent reader

ADVANCED READING
Short paragraphs, chapters, and exciting themes for the perfect bridge to chapter books

I Can Read Books have introduced children to the joy of reading since 1957. Featuring award-winning authors and illustrators and a fabulous cast of beloved characters, I Can Read Books set the standard for beginning readers.

A lifetime of discovery begins with the magical words **"I Can Read!"**

Visit www.icanread.com for information on enriching your child's reading experience.

I Can Read!

Shared My First Reading

Biscuit

story by ALYSSA SATIN CAPUCILLI
pictures by PAT SCHORIES

HarperCollins*Publishers*

HarperCollins®, ☛®, and I Can Read Book® are trademarks of HarperCollins Publishers Inc.

Biscuit Text copyright © 1996 by Alyssa Satin Capucilli Illustrations copyright © 1996 by Pat Schories All rights reserved. No part of this book may be used or reproduced in any manner whatsoever without written permission except in the case of brief quotations embodied in critical articles and reviews. Manufactured in China. For information address HarperCollins Children's Books, a division of HarperCollins Publishers, 195 Broadway, New York, NY 10007. www.harperchildrens.com

Library of Congress Cataloging-in-Publication Data
Capucilli, Alyssa Satin.
  Biscuit / story by Alyssa Satin Capucilli ; pictures by Pat Schories.
    p. cm. — (An I can read book)
  Summary: A little yellow dog wants ever one more thing before he'll go to sleep.
  ISBN-10: 0-06-026197-8 (trade bdg.) — ISBN-13: 978-0-06-026197-9 (trade bdg.)
  ISBN-10: 0-06-026198-6 (lib. bdg.) — ISBN-13: 978-0-06-026198-6 (lib. bdg.)
  ISBN-10: 0-06-444212-8 (pbk.) — ISBN-13: 978-0-06-444212-1 (pbk.)
  [1. Dogs—Fiction. 2. Bedtime—Fiction.] I. Schories, Pat, ill. II. Title. III. Series.
PZ7.C179Bi 1997   95-9716
[E]—dc20   CIP
                                                                AC

19 20 SCP 100 99 98 97 96 95

*For Laura and Peter who wait patiently
for a Biscuit of their very own*
—A. S. C.

For Tess
—P. S.

This is Biscuit.

Biscuit is small.

Biscuit is yellow.

Time for bed, Biscuit!

Woof, woof!

Biscuit wants to play.

Time for bed, Biscuit!

Woof, woof!

Biscuit wants a snack.

Time for bed, Biscuit!

Woof, woof!

Biscuit wants a drink.

Time for bed, Biscuit!

Woof, woof!

Biscuit wants to hear a story.

Time for bed, Biscuit!

Woof, woof!

Biscuit wants his blanket.

Time for bed, Biscuit!

Woof, woof!

Biscuit wants his doll.

Time for bed, Biscuit!

Woof, woof!

Biscuit wants a hug.

Time for bed, Biscuit!

Woof, woof!

Biscuit wants a kiss.

Time for bed, Biscuit!

Woof, woof!

Biscuit wants a light on.

Woof!

Biscuit wants to be tucked in.

Woof!

Biscuit wants one more kiss.

Woof!

Biscuit wants one more hug.

Woof!

Biscuit wants to curl up.

Sleepy puppy.

Good night, Biscuit.

Dear Parent:
Your child's love of reading starts here!

Every child learns to read in a different way and at his or her own speed. Some go back and forth between reading levels and read favorite books again and again. Others read through each level in order. You can help your young reader improve and become more confident by encouraging his or her own interests and abilities. From books your child reads with you to the first books he or she reads alone, there are I Can Read Books for every stage of reading:

SHARED READING
Basic language, word repetition, and whimsical illustrations, ideal for sharing with your emergent reader

BEGINNING READING
Short sentences, familiar words, and simple concepts for children eager to read on their own

READING WITH HELP
Engaging stories, longer sentences, and language play for developing readers

READING ALONE
Complex plots, challenging vocabulary, and high-interest topics for the independent reader

ADVANCED READING
Short paragraphs, chapters, and exciting themes for the perfect bridge to chapter books

I Can Read Books have introduced children to the joy of reading since 1957. Featuring award-winning authors and illustrators and a fabulous cast of beloved characters, I Can Read Books set the standard for beginning readers.

A lifetime of discovery begins with the magical words **"I Can Read!"**

Visit www.icanread.com for information on enriching your child's reading experience.

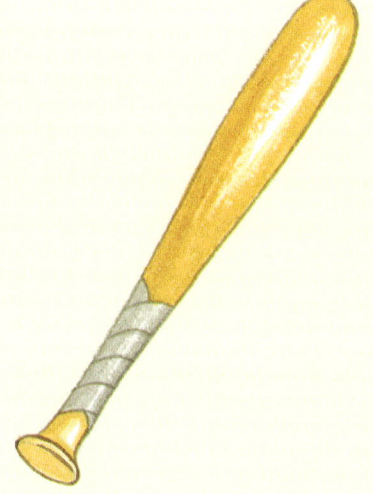
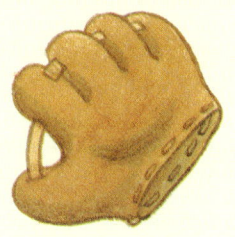

For Peter and Laura
—A.S.C.

For Alyssa,
for all the wonderful stories
that let me do what I do
—P.S.

I Can Read Book® is a trademark of HarperCollins Publishers.

Biscuit Plays Ball
Text copyright © 2012 by Alyssa Satin Capucilli
Illustrations copyright © 2012 by Pat Schories
All rights reserved. Manufactured in China. No part of this book may be used or reproduced in any manner whatsoever without written permission except in the case of brief quotations embodied in critical articles and reviews. For information address HarperCollins Children's Books, a division of HarperCollins Publishers, 195 Broadway, New York, NY 10007.
www.icanread.com

Library of Congress Cataloging-in-Publication Data is available.
ISBN 978-0-06-193503-9 (trade bdg.) — ISBN 978-0-06-193502-2 (pbk.)

21 SCP 10 9 8 7   ❖   First Edition

Biscuit Plays Ball

story by ALYSSA SATIN CAPUCILLI
pictures by PAT SCHORIES

HARPER
An Imprint of HarperCollinsPublishers

It's time to play ball, Biscuit.

Woof, woof!

Look, Biscuit.

The game is about to begin.

Woof, woof!

Stay here now, Biscuit.

You can watch.

Woof, woof!

Wait, Biscuit.

Where are you going?

Woof!

You can't play ball now, Biscuit.

There are no dogs
in this ball game.

Stay here, Biscuit.

Woof, woof!

Uh-oh, Biscuit.

Not again!
Woof, woof!

Come along, Biscuit.
There are no dogs
in this ball game.

Won't you stay here, Biscuit?
Woof, woof!

Biscuit does not want to stay.
Woof, woof!

Biscuit wants to play, too.
Woof!

Biscuit wants to run.
Woof!

Biscuit wants to jump.
Woof!

Biscuit wants to play ball!
Woof, woof!

Oh no, Biscuit.

Come back with the ball!

Silly puppy.

How can we play now?

Woof, woof! Woof, woof!

Bow wow!

Oh, Biscuit!

You found your friend Puddles.

And Puddles has a ball, too!

Woof, woof!

Bow wow!

It's time to play ball, Biscuit.

Time for all of us!
Woof!

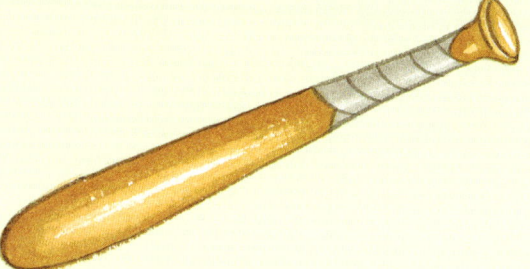

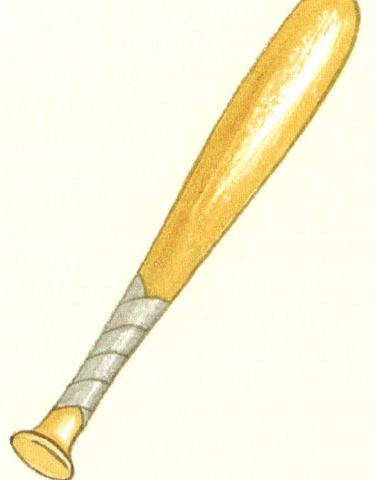

Dear Parent:
Your child's love of reading starts here!

Every child learns to read in a different way and at his or her own speed. Some go back and forth between reading levels and read favorite books again and again. Others read through each level in order. You can help your young reader improve and become more confident by encouraging his or her own interests and abilities. From books your child reads with you to the first books he or she reads alone, there are I Can Read Books for every stage of reading:

SHARED READING
Basic language, word repetition, and whimsical illustrations, ideal for sharing with your emergent reader

BEGINNING READING
Short sentences, familiar words, and simple concepts for children eager to read on their own

READING WITH HELP
Engaging stories, longer sentences, and language play for developing readers

READING ALONE
Complex plots, challenging vocabulary, and high-interest topics for the independent reader

I Can Read Books have introduced children to the joy of reading since 1957. Featuring award-winning authors and illustrators and a fabulous cast of beloved characters, I Can Read Books set the standard for beginning readers.

A lifetime of discovery begins with the magical words **"I Can Read!"**

*Visit www.icanread.com for information
on enriching your child's reading experience.*

*For Peter and Laura,
who love to go camping
under the stars!*
—A.S.C.

I Can Read® and I Can Read Book® are trademarks of HarperCollins Publishers.

Biscuit Goes Camping Text copyright © 2015 by Alyssa Satin Capucilli Illustrations copyright © 2015 by Pat Schories All rights reserved. Printed in China. No part of this book may be used or reproduced in any manner whatsoever without written permission except in the case of brief quotations embodied in critical articles and reviews. For information address HarperCollins Children's a division of HarperCollins Publishers, 195 Broadway, New York, NY 10007.
www.icanread.com

ISBN 978-0-06-223693-7 (pbk.) — ISBN 978-0-06-223694-4 (trade bdg.)

The artist used traditional watercolor and Photoshop to create the digital illustrations for this book.

22   SCP   23   ❖

Biscuit Goes Camping

story by ALYSSA SATIN CAPUCILLI
pictures by PAT SCHORIES

HARPER
An Imprint of HarperCollinsPublishers

This way, Biscuit.

It's time to go camping.

Woof, woof!

We have our tent.

Woof!

We have our flashlight
and blankets, too.
Woof, woof!

Silly puppy!
No tugging.

It's time to go camping.
Woof!

Wait, Biscuit.

What have you found?

Woof, woof!

Croak!

You found a frog, Biscuit.

Woof, woof!

Whoo-oo! Whoo-oo!

Funny puppy.

It's only the wind, Biscuit.

There are so many
new sights and sounds
when you go camping.
Woof!

Oh, Biscuit!

What have you found now?

Woof, woof!

Blink! Blink!
It's a firefly, Biscuit.
The firefly says
good night.

It's time for us to say good night, too, Biscuit.

Curl up, Biscuit.
Woof, woof!

Crack! Crack!
Boom! Boom!

Oh no!

Here comes the rain!

How can we go camping now?

Woof, woof!
Woof, woof!
Biscuit! Wait for me!

Woof!

Smart puppy!

You found the perfect place to go camping.

Blink! Blink!

Woof, woof!

Good night, Biscuit.

Dear Parent:
Your child's love of reading starts here!

Every child learns to read in a different way and at his or her own speed. Some go back and forth between reading levels and read favorite books again and again. Others read through each level in order. You can help your young reader improve and become more confident by encouraging his or her own interests and abilities. From books your child reads with you to the first books he or she reads alone, there are I Can Read Books for every stage of reading:

SHARED READING
Basic language, word repetition, and whimsical illustrations, ideal for sharing with your emergent reader

BEGINNING READING
Short sentences, familiar words, and simple concepts for children eager to read on their own

READING WITH HELP
Engaging stories, longer sentences, and language play for developing readers

READING ALONE
Complex plots, challenging vocabulary, and high-interest topics for the independent reader

ADVANCED READING
Short paragraphs, chapters, and exciting themes for the perfect bridge to chapter books

I Can Read Books have introduced children to the joy of reading since 1957. Featuring award-winning authors and illustrators and a fabulous cast of beloved characters, I Can Read Books set the standard for beginning readers.

A lifetime of discovery begins with the magical words **"I Can Read!"**

*Visit www.icanread.com for information
on enriching your child's reading experience.*

*For James, who loves to help
feed the pets!
—A.S.C.*

I Can Read Book® is a trademark of HarperCollins Publishers.

Biscuit Feeds the Pets   Text copyright © 2016 by Alyssa Satin Capucilli Illustrations copyright © 2016 by Pat Schories
All rights reserved. Manufactured in China. No part of this book may be used or reproduced in any manner whatsoever without written permission except in the case of brief quotations embodied in critical articles and reviews. For information address HarperCollins Children's Books, a division of HarperCollins Publishers, 195 Broadway, New York, NY 10007.
www.icanread.com

Library of Congress Control Number: 2014041211
ISBN 978-0-06-223697-5 (hardcover) — ISBN 978-0-06-223696-8 (pbk.)

The artist used traditional watercolor to create the illustrations for this book.

22   SCP   20 19   ❖   First Edition

Biscuit Feeds the Pets

story by ALYSSA SATIN CAPUCILLI
pictures by PAT SCHORIES

HARPER
An Imprint of HarperCollinsPublishers

Here, Biscuit.
We're going to help
Mrs. Gray today.
Woof, woof!

We're going to help feed the pets!

Are you ready, Biscuit?
Woof, woof!

We can help feed
the fish, Biscuit.

We can help feed
the kittens, too.
Woof, woof!
Meow!

Wait, Biscuit!
Where are you going?

Woof, woof!
Yip—yip—yip!

Oh, Biscuit.

You found the new puppies!

Woof!

This way, Biscuit.

Woof, woof!

There are more pets
to feed over here.

Come out of there.

It's not time to play.

It's time to help Mrs. Gray.

Woof!

Yip!

Oh no, Biscuit!

Come back.
How will we feed
the pets now?

Woof, woof!
Yip—yip—yip!
Meow!

No, Biscuit, no.
Not the water bowl!

SPLASH!
Silly puppies!

Woof, woof!
Yip—yip—yip!

Funny puppy!

You found your own way to help feed the pets, Biscuit.

You made lots of
new friends, too!

Meow!

Yip—yip—yip!

Woof, woof!

Dear Parent:
Your child's love of reading starts here!

Every child learns to read in a different way and at his or her own speed. Some go back and forth between reading levels and read favorite books again and again. Others read through each level in order. You can help your young reader improve and become more confident by encouraging his or her own interests and abilities. From books your child reads with you to the first books he or she reads alone, there are I Can Read Books for every stage of reading:

SHARED READING
Basic language, word repetition, and whimsical illustrations, ideal for sharing with your emergent reader

BEGINNING READING
Short sentences, familiar words, and simple concepts for children eager to read on their own

READING WITH HELP
Engaging stories, longer sentences, and language play for developing readers

READING ALONE
Complex plots, challenging vocabulary, and high-interest topics for the independent reader

ADVANCED READING
Short paragraphs, chapters, and exciting themes for the perfect bridge to chapter books

I Can Read Books have introduced children to the joy of reading since 1957. Featuring award-winning authors and illustrators and a fabulous cast of beloved characters, I Can Read Books set the standard for beginning readers.

A lifetime of discovery begins with the magical words **"I Can Read!"**

Visit www.icanread.com for information
on enriching your child's reading experience.

*For Elliot Jude Chaplin,
and for our beloved librarian
friends who share the love of
reading with all of us!*
—A.S.C. and P.S.

I Can Read Book® is a trademark of HarperCollins Publishers.

Biscuit Loves the Library Text copyright © 2014 by Alyssa Satin Capucilli Illustrations copyright © 2014 by Pat Schories
All rights reserved. Manufactured in China. No part of this book may be used or reproduced in any manner whatsoever without written permission except in the case of brief quotations embodied in critical articles and reviews. For information address HarperCollins Children's Books, a division of HarperCollins Publishers, 195 Broadway, New York, NY 10007.
www.icanread.com

ISBN 978-0-06-193507-7 (trade bdg.) — ISBN 978-0-06-193506-0 (pbk.)

20 SCP 27 ❖ First Edition

Biscuit Loves the Library

story by ALYSSA SATIN CAPUCILLI
pictures by PAT SCHORIES

HARPER
An Imprint of HarperCollinsPublishers

It's a very special day at the library, Biscuit. Woof, woof!

It's Read to a Pet Day!
I can read to you,
Biscuit.
Woof, woof!

Come along, Biscuit.

Let's find a book.

Woof, woof!

See, Biscuit?
There are books
about bunnies and bears.
Woof, woof!

And big dinosaurs, too!
Woof!

Funny puppy!
That's not a real bone!
Woof, woof!

Look, Biscuit.

There are more books over here.

Woof, woof!

Biscuit! Where are you?
Woof!

You found the puppets, Biscuit.

Woof, woof!
And you even found
stories we can listen to.
Woof!

Now, which book will it be?

Woof, woof!

Biscuit! Wait for me!

Woof!

Oh, Biscuit!

You found the librarian
and a book that's just right.
Woof, woof!

You found a cozy spot
filled with friends, too.

Everyone loves the library, Biscuit.

Woof, woof!

Let's read!

Woof!